TAKE TEN YEARS

1900s
The First Decade

Library of Congress Cataloging-in-Publication Data

Sharman, Margaret.
  1900s / Margaret Sharman.
    p.   cm. — (Take ten years)
  Includes bibliographical references and index.
  Summary: Explores the decade of the 1900s worldwide, a time which
included the Wright brothers' first successful flight at Kitty Hawk,
a Nobel Prize for Marie Curie and her husband, and the end of the
Victorian era.
  ISBN 0-8114-3073-1
  1. History, Modern—20th century—Juvenile literature.
[1. History, Modern—20th century.]   I. Title.   II. Title: Nineteen
hundreds.   III. Series.
D422.S53 1994   93-12034
909.82—dc20   CIP
                                                        AC

Typeset by Multifacit Graphics, Keyport, NJ
Printed in Spain by GRAFO, S.A., Bilbao
Bound in the United States by Lake Book, Melrose Park, IL
1 2 3 4 5 6 7 8 9 0 LB 99 98 97 96 95 94

Acknowledgments

Maps — Jillian Luff, Bitmap Graphics
Design — Neil Sayer
Editor — Caroline Sheldrick

For permission to reproduce copyright material the author and publishers gratefully acknowledge the following:

Cover photographs — (left) The Bettmann Archive; (top to bottom) The Bettmann Archive, The Bettmann Archive, Culver Pictures, Inc., Library of Congress

page 4 — (from top), e.t. archive, The Vintage Magazine Co., Mary Evans Picture Library, Mary Evans Picture Library, Mary Evans Picture Library, Culver Pictures, Inc.; page 5— (from top) Popperfoto, The Illustrated London News Picture Library, Popperfoto, Mary Evans Picture Library, Mary Evans Picture Library; page 9 (top) Culver Pictures, Inc., (bottom) The Vintage Magazine Co.; page 10 — (top) Popperfoto, (bottom) Mary Evans Picture Library; page 11 — (top) UPI/Bettmann, (bottom) The Vintage Magazine Co.; page 12 — The Vintage Magazine Co.; page 13 — (left) e.t. archive, (right) Mary Evans Picture Library/Explorer; page 14 — The Bettmann Archive; page 15 — (top) e.t. archive, (bottom) The Bettmann Archive; page 16 — National Library of Medicine; page 17 — (top) The Vintage Magazine Co., (bottom) The Bettmann Archive; page 18 — (top) Mary Evans Picture Library, (center) e.t. archive, (bottom) The Vintage Magazine Co.; page 19 — The Vintage Magazine Co.; page 20 — (left) Mary Evans Picture Library, (right) The Bettmann Archive; page 21 — (left) Culver Pictures, Inc., (right) Mary Evans Picture Library; page 22 — (left) Mary Evans Picture Library, (center) Tate Gallery, London/Bridgeman Art Library, (right) Mary Evans Picture Library; page 24 — (left) Culver Pictures, Inc.; (right) Mary Evans Picture Library; page 25 — (top) Mary Evans Picture Library, (bottom) Culver Pictures, Inc.; page 26 — Mary Evans Picture Library; page 27 — (left) The Vintage Magazine Co., (right) The Bettmann Archive; page 28 — (left) The Vintage Magazine Co., (right) Culver Pictures, Inc.; page 29 — Culver Pictures, Inc.; page 30 — Popperfoto; page 31 — (top) The Vintage Magazine Co., (bottom) Mary Evans Picture Library; page 33 — (top) Culver Pictures, Inc., (bottom) e.t. archive; page 34 — (left) Culver Pictures, Inc., (right) Mary Evans Picture Library; page 35 — The Illustrated London News Picture Library; page 36 — Mary Evans Picture Library; page 37 — (top) The Bettmann Archive, (bottom) Mary Evans Picture Library; page 38 — (top) The Vintage Magazine Co., (bottom) Popperfoto; page 39 — Mary Evans Picture Library; page 40 — (left) The Illustrated London News Picture Library, (right) The Hulton Picture Company; page 41 — e.t. archive; page 42 — (left and right) Mary Evans Picture Library; page 43 — (left) The Bettmann Archive, (right) Mary Evans Picture Library; page 44 — (from top) Mary Evans Picture Library, Mary Evans Picture Library, Mary Evans Picture Library, The Vintage Magazine Co., Mary Evans Picture Library; page 45 — (from top) The Advertising Archives, The Vintage Magazine Co., The Vintage Magazine Co., Mary Evans Picture Library, Mary Evans Picture Library.

TAKE TEN YEARS

1900s
The First Decade

MARGARET SHARMAN

RSVP
RAINTREE
STECK-VAUGHN
P U B L I S H E R S
The Steck-Vaughn Company

Austin, Texas

Contents

The pictures on page 4 show
British troops in the Boer War
Paris exhibition 1900
Queen Victoria
The czar of Russia, Nicholas II, with his family
President Theodore Roosevelt

The pictures on page 5 show
City Hall, San Francisco, damaged by the 1906 earthquake
A church damaged by riots in Spain
Robert Peary, explorer, with his wife and son
Turks in Constantinople, during the revolution
Louis Blériot lands at Dover

Introduction

In the first ten years of the twentieth century, many political events involved colonies or territories belonging to European powers. In 1901 Australia became part of the British Empire. When the Boer War ended in 1902, South Africa was added to the huge empire. The British were proud of their empire, and said "the sun never sets on it" because it stretched around the world. The British government sought to protect empire trade by taxing imports from other countries.

Some colonies did not want to be ruled from overseas. The Ashanti of the Gold Coast in Africa almost succeeded in killing the British governor and his wife. The Germans faced an uprising in Tanganyika. In other parts of Africa, Morocco became a French mandate; and the misrule in the Belgian Congo was exposed.

In Europe, two Balkan states left the Turkish Empire, and a new political party started the reform of Turkey. The Germans, French, and British all tried to win spheres of influence, as they struggled for a balance of power. By 1909 Britain and Germany were arming as if for war.

Mount Vesuvius in Italy, and Mount Pelée in the Caribbean both erupted. There were major earthquakes in the United States, South America, and Sicily; hundreds of people died. Those who were made homeless added to the great number of poor and starving people in the world.

At this time America was everyone's idea of heaven. If things were bad in Russia, the Balkans, Ireland, or Japan, people thought about emigrating to what they saw as the land of opportunity. The boat fare was cheap, and immigrants thought that jobs were easy to get. This was not always so.

There was certainly a difference between rich and poor in the United States. However, it was also true that there did exist great opportunity for people to improve their lives in this country. Through hard work, education, and determination many poor people were able to make remarkable gains. Thousands of immigrants achieved what later became known as the "American Dream."

YEARS	WORLD AFFAIRS
1900	International force relieves Peking.
1901	U.S. to govern Philippines Australia joins British Empire. Chinese to pay for Boxer rebellion
1902	Nations look for "spheres of influence."
1903	Panama becomes independent.
1904	*Entente cordiale* between France and Britain
1905	Russians ally with Germany.
1906	Morocco to be French mandate
1907	Belgium government buys Congo Free State from Belgian king Leopold II.
1908	Turkish sultan forced to appoint parliament. Crisis in the Balkans
1909	Serbia and Austria avoid conflict, but Balkans remain tense.

WARS & CIVIL DISORDER	PEOPLE	EVENTS
Boer War in South Africa Boxer rebellion in China	Davis and Ward win Davis Cup. Eugene Debs to run for presidency	Paris Exhibition held. Hawaii becomes U.S. territory.
	Queen Victoria dies. President McKinley shot. Tolstoy criticizes Russian government.	Oil found in Texas. Theodore Roosevelt becomes President. Marconi sends signal by wireless.
Boer War ends.	Kipling writes *Just So Stories*. Emile Zola dies.	Control of yellow fever begins. Mount Pelée erupts. The Aswan Dam is opened.
King and queen of Serbia murdered.	Marie and Pierre Curie win Nobel Prize Wright brothers take to the air. James Whistler, artist, dies.	New pope crowned in Rome.
War between Japan and Russia	Robert Falcon Scott lectures on Antarctica. Theodore Roosevelt reelected President.	British expedition to Tibet Olympic Games in United States St. Louis Exposition opens.
Revolution in Russia Japan wins war in Far East.	Father George Gapon leads demonstrators to Winter Palace in Russia.	German kaiser visits Morocco. Jews celebrate 250 years in America.
Rebellion in Tanganyika suppressed.	Alfred Dreyfus receives Legion of Honor. President Roosevelt wins Nobel Peace Prize.	Mount Vesuvius erupts. San Francisco almost destroyed by earthquake.
French vineyard workers riot over wine prices.	Mohandas Gandhi leads Indian protest in South Africa. Florence Nightingale honored. Clarence Darrow defends "Big Bill" Haywood in Chicago.	*Lusitania* breaks transatlantic crossing speed record. Suffragettes stage rally in N.Y.
Britain and Germany in arms race	Taft elected President. Ford produces first Model T. Sir Arthur Evans discovers Knossos.	Olympic Games in London Earthquake in Sicily
Riots in Spain Young Turks take over in Turkey.	Peary and Henson reach North Pole. Blériot flies Channel. Rutherford wins Nobel Prize.	World's largest skyscraper built in New York City. Population of U.S. reaches 92 million.

1900

Jan. 25   Boers win the Battle of Spion Kop
April 30   Fifth Paris Exhibition in full swing
June 14   Hawaii becomes a U.S. territory
July 22   Olympic Games end
Aug. 14   Boxer rebellion defeated in China

THE BOER WAR

BOERS TRAP BRITISH IN THREE TOWNS

Jan. 6, Ladysmith, South Africa The British and the Boers (Dutch settlers, or Afrikaaners) both have provinces in South Africa. The Transvaal, a Boer province, has rich gold mines, where many British men are employed. The Boers tax them heavily, and the British government has objected. This is one of the quarrels that have caused this war. British troops have arrived from England, and both sides have suffered many casualties in the fighting.

The Boers have surrounded Ladysmith, the British military headquarters, and two other towns, Mafeking and Kimberley. Thousands of British soldiers and civilians, both black and white, are trapped in these towns. They are now short of food.

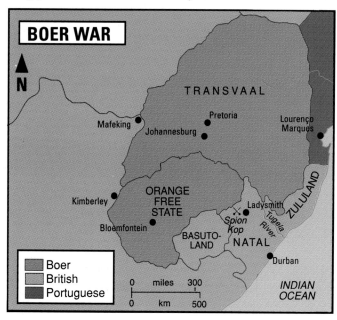

BLOODY BATTLE ON SPION KOP

Jan. 25, Spion Kop, Natal Last night, after dark, 2,000 British soldiers swarmed up a hill called Spion Kop, overlooking a tributary of the Tugela River. With their field guns they hoped to guard their troops as they crossed the river and marched towards Ladysmith, 16 miles (25 kilometers) away. But at daylight they were shocked to find that the Boers were on a higher spur of the hill. High explosive shells burst among them all day. As night fell, the remaining British soldiers retreated to the valley. Over 1,500 men have died today on Spion Kop. Winston Churchill, a war correspondent, said: "Men were staggering along alone, or supported by comrades, or crawling on hands and knees, or carried on stretchers . . . I passed about two hundred as I was climbing up."

BRITISH ENTER MAFEKING

May 16, Mafeking British troops have ended the Boers' siege of Kimberley and Ladysmith. Today they marched into Mafeking. This little railway town was besieged by the Boers for seven months. The colonel in charge of the town, Robert Baden-Powell, has kept the enemy guessing. One of his deceptions was to make imitation guns out of wood. Young boys carrying these wooden guns marched around the town walls. From the Boer positions the weapons looked real, and they thought Mafeking was well defended.

The Boer War or South African War began in 1899. It is being fought by Dutch settlers, the Boers, against the English.

CONSTRUCTION BEGINS ON SUBWAY

March 24, New York Using a sterling silver spade, New York City Mayor Robert A. Van Wyck today dug the first shovelful of dirt to begin the construction of an underground railroad system. When the system is completed at an expected cost of $36 million, it will link Manhattan with its neighboring borough to the southeast, Brooklyn. The tunnel that the mayor began today marks the start of an ambitious plan to link Manhattan by rail with New Jersey and Staten Island as well.

Mayor Van Wyck (left front) and other officials leave City Hall for the ground-breaking ceremony of the new underground railroad.

FOREIGNERS' ORDEAL IN CHINA

BOXERS KILL DIPLOMATS

June 20, Peking, China The German minister to China was today murdered in Peking. This follows the killing nine days ago of the Japanese chancellor. Members of a Chinese secret society are murdering foreigners and Chinese Christians. Europeans call these killers "the Boxers," because of the rebels' belief that boxing and other exercises protect them from bullets.

The Chinese empress T'zu-hsi approves of their actions. She, too, wants to get rid of "foreign devils." She has sent Chinese troops to besiege the legations. These diplomatic buildings are like a foreign walled town within Peking. About 900 foreign diplomats, their wives and their children, and 3,000 Chinese Christians, are trapped there. All day the Boxers and Chinese troops shoot over the walls, and set fire to legation buildings. The besieged people are living on starvation rations. Every day they have to put out fires, build temporary shelters, and care for the wounded.

An army of European, American, and Japanese soldiers has set off from the coast by train to help them. They are due to arrive tonight.

SIEGE ENDS AS ARMY ARRIVES

Aug. 14, Peking On June 21 the empress declared war on all foreigners. Chinese soldiers destroyed a troop train at Tientsin, and the soldiers had to fight their way to Peking on foot. They have arrived just in time. In another day the Boxers would have broken into the legations. The empress has fled from Peking. An eyewitness in one legation said: "By two o'clock every rifle that could be brought in line was replying to the enemy's fire. If this continued, in a couple of hours our ammunition would be exhausted, and we would have only our bayonets to rely on."

Italian soldiers guard Boxer prisoners. A combined European, American, and Japanese army has put down the rebellion.

The fantasy "illuminated palace" on a lake is a feature of the exhibition.

LIGHTS DRAW CROWDS

April 30, Paris, France Buildings, fountains, and the Seine River have all been lit with the recently invented electric lighting for two weeks now, to celebrate the Fifth Paris Exhibition. Many countries have put on displays. There is an English Tudor house, an Indian pavilion, and a Chinese pagoda. The exhibition also reminds us of all the wonderful inventions, arts, and buildings of the last century. These include the Eiffel Tower, now ten years old. Already people are saying that this will be "the exhibition of the century."

FRENCH DOMINATE OLYMPICS

July 22, Paris The Olympic Games ended today. They were part of the Paris Exhibition. Events took place on bumpy grass and dirt roads. They were so informal that some of the winners did not realize they were competing in the Olympics; and a Dutch rowing crew invited a small French boy to act as coxswain, though he had never coxed before.

The French team was the largest, with 884 competitors. They won the greatest number of medals. The United States sent their college and club teams. Ray Ewry of the United States was outstanding at the high and long jump. Women competed for golf and tennis medals.

The 500-meter run takes place between trees and onlookers in a park in Paris.

HAWAII NOW A U.S. TERRITORY

June 14, Hawaii This chain of islands, located near the center of the North Pacific Ocean, today officially became a territory of the United States. President William McKinley has supported territorial status for Hawaii. He argued that the region provided a natural gateway for trade in the Far East, and might also be a strategic military position. The first governor of the territory will be Sanford B. Dole, who had been president of the republic of Hawaii.

ZEPPELIN'S AIRSHIP MAKES FLIGHT

July 20, Berlin, Germany An airship designed and built by Count Ferdinand von Zeppelin made its first flight today near Friedrichshafen. Its cloth-covered hull contains 16 hydrogen-filled gas cells and two 16-horsepower engines. It can travel at a top speed of 17 miles (27 km) per hour.

The United States flag waves over Hawaii's royal palace.

NEWS IN BRIEF . . .

DAVIS RECEIVES HIS OWN TROPHY

Aug. 10, Boston The American tennis players Dwight Davis and Holcombe Ward have won the first Davis Cup tournament. This is the competition that winner Dwight Davis himself set up six months ago!

DEBS TO RUN FOR PRESIDENCY

March 6, Indianapolis Eugene V. Debs, a labor leader and former member of the Indiana legislature, has announced that he will run for President. Debs, 45, will run as the candidate of the Social Democratic party, which he helped found. He is hoping for broad support from labor groups.

MORE HORSELESS CARRIAGES MANUFACTURED

Dec. 1, New York The United States now has 8,000 cars on the roads. Over 1,600 motor cars, driven by steam power, were manufactured this year. Another 1,500 electric cars were on sale. And a new fuel, gasoline, is increasingly being used.

Two designs of electric car.

1901

THE QUEEN IS DEAD
END OF AN ERA

Jan. 22, Osborne, Isle of Wight The "Victorian Age" is over. This morning Queen Victoria of England died at Osborne House on the Isle of Wight. She was 81. Few of her subjects can remember any other monarch, as she has ruled since 1837.

HORSES BREAK FREE AT FUNERAL

Feb. 2, Windsor, England The queen's coffin arrived on this cold and windy morning by boat and train from the Isle of Wight. At Windsor railway station it was put on a gun carriage. But one of the horses pulling the carriage reared up, and then both horses broke free. The naval guards had to pull the gun carriage to Windsor Castle Chapel. Thousands of people lined the route. The chapel bell tolled, and guns were fired at one-minute intervals. At the end of the service an official cried, "God Save the King!" A new era has begun.

"It was eerie entering the half-dark Choir lit only by wax tapers—for it was a dull day—as we moved up to the altar rails, taking our places on the north side. From here we could see the Royal Box, in which were Queen Alexandra and the other Royal ladies in deep mourning . . . I received an official fee of half-a-crown [2s 6d] for singing, and with it I bought a photograph of the old Queen."

Reminiscences of a Windsor choirboy

CARNEGIE TO GIVE AWAY FORTUNE

March 13, Pittsburgh Steel baron Andrew Carnegie announced his retirement today, adding that he intends to spend it giving away his fortune of more than $300 million. In a letter addressed to "the good people of Pittsburgh," the city where he made his money, Carnegie also said that he would set up a fund for old and disabled employees of his steel company. The industrialist, who came to the United States as a penniless Scottish immigrant, became a millionaire in his twenties.

ATTACK SHOCKS AMERICA

PRESIDENT SHOT

Sept. 6, Buffalo, New York In front of a shocked audience, President William McKinley was shot at as he held out his hand to his attacker. The President had been speaking on the need to trade with other countries. "Isolation is no longer possible or desirable," he said. After his speech people lined up to shake his hand. Among them was Leon Czolgosz, son of a Polish immigrant. He fired twice at the President, whose condition tonight is not thought to be serious.

President William McKinley is shot at close range by Leon Czolgosz.

ROOSEVELT SWORN IN

Sept. 14, Buffalo, New York Vice-President Theodore Roosevelt was on a hunting holiday when he received news that President McKinley was dying from gunshot wounds. Today he has become, at 42, the youngest President of the United States.

AUTHOR BLAMED FOR RIOTS

March 17, St. Petersburg, Russia Leo Tolstoy, the author of *War and Peace*, is blamed for serious student riots in Moscow and St. Petersburg. Tolstoy has written against the government and against religion. Last year the Orthodox Church excommunicated him. Today the students were beaten back by mounted troops, the Cossacks, and hundreds have been arrested.

Leo Tolstoy.

U.S. SENDS GOVERNOR TO PHILIPPINES

July 4, Manila Judge William Howard Taft is the new governor of the Philippines. For the past two years American troops have fought a guerrilla war against Filipinos, natives of the Philippines, who object to being part of an American colony. The Anti-Imperialist League in the U.S. agrees with the Filipinos that no country should be ruled by another without its consent. The Filipino rebel leader Emilio Aguinaldo was captured in the mountains in May. Since then our troops have been withdrawn. Governor Taft is a sympathetic man, and is winning friends on the islands.

BOER CAMPS A DISGRACE

Aug. 16, Cape Town The Boers in South Africa continue to fight guerrilla battles against British soldiers. Civilians, mainly women and children, have been providing Boers with food and clothing. To stop this, Lord Kitchener, commander of the British forces, ordered that all civilians should be put into guarded camps. Many of their farms have been burned, and the fields are full of dead animals, shot by British soldiers.

The camps are terrible places. There are no doctors or medical supplies, no blankets, and no proper sanitation. Water is very scarce. The inmates get less food than the soldiers do. Many are starving, and hundreds die from disease. People from Britain who have visited the camps are shocked by the conditions in which the Boers have to live.

CHINESE TO PAY FOR BOXER REBELLION

Sept. 7, Peking The Chinese government has been ordered to pay a huge sum to the countries that raised the siege of Peking last year. American authorities say that half the money they receive will go to help Chinese students in the United States.

In China, two princes and three leading courtiers will be beheaded, and three officials have been ordered to commit suicide. Over a hundred other people will be punished. Empress T'zu-hsi will continue as ruler. The Chinese feel humiliated by the affair.

DISASTROUS FIRE IN FLORIDA

May 3, Jacksonville The worst fire in this city's history has caused $15 million in damages to property and left more than 10,000 people without homes. A defective wire at a factory is thought to have been the cause of the blaze. More than 1,000 houses were destroyed in about 130 blocks. Shops, theaters, hotels, and churches also burned. The fire was fanned by fierce winds and could not immediately be contained. It finally died out after about 10 hours. It is not yet known how many people were killed or hurt.

BUSINESSMEN WARNED BY PRESIDENT

Dec. 3, Washington President Roosevelt has spoken out against "trusts" in American business. Trusts are formed when businesses join together and have a monopoly on the goods they sell. The trust can then fix prices and wages because there is no competition. The President says trusts destroy small businesses. They also make a few men very rich. Trusts have been growing in power.

U.S. WINS AMERICA'S CUP AGAIN

Oct. 4, New Jersey Sailing home two seconds ahead of the British challenger *Shamrock* off the coast of New Jersey, the American yacht *Columbia* won the coveted America's Cup. Sir Thomas Lipton, skipper of the *Shamrock*, had his hopes of a comeback crushed after rebuilding his vessel when it was wrecked last year. The America's Cup race began in 1851 when the U.S. yacht *America* bested a British ship in a race around the Isle of Wight in the English channel.

NEWS IN BRIEF . . .

NEW COMMONWEALTH COUNTRY BORN

Jan. 1, Sydney Australia enters the new century as the youngest commonwealth country in the British Empire—born today! Six Australian states have joined in a federal union. This is the first time in history that a whole continent has been occupied by one nation. Celebrations in this city began with a procession through the streets to a pavilion. Here a message from Queen Victoria was read out.

NEGRO LEADER TO VISIT WHITE HOUSE

Nov. 16, Washington President Roosevelt has stirred up a great deal of angry discussion. He has invited Negro leader Booker T. Washington to visit the White House. Washington has advised Negroes to stop asking for equality and concentrate on getting better jobs. This advice has been criticized by many Negroes. Now Roosevelt is receiving criticism for inviting Washington to the White House.

A LAND BATHED IN OIL

Jan. 10, Beaumont, Texas The oil that seeped out of the ground in Texas and spoiled crops is going to transform the country. Oil drillers today bored through rock and came to a layer of oil underneath. It rushed up to the surface in a great black fountain, shooting high into the sky. When it is under control, it will provide fuel for years to come, and make Texas rich.

MARCONI'S MAGIC MOMENT MAY LEAD TO MORE

Dec. 16, Poldhu, Cornwall The Italian inventor Guglielmo Marconi has made a great advance. He has succeeded in sending a signal by wireless telegraphy right across the Atlantic Ocean. The signal traveled rapidly from Cornwall, England, to Newfoundland, Canada, a distance of over 2,000 miles (3,300 km). The sound Mr. Marconi received was faint, but there is no doubt that his theory of transmitting messages through the air works.

The inventor Guglielmo Marconi and his wireless apparatus.

1902

NEW CONTROLS FOR DANGEROUS DISEASE

Feb. 22, Havana, Cuba A scientific report was published today by the U.S. Army Yellow Fever Commission. It officially agrees with the theory of Cuban doctor Carlos J. Finlay about the cause of the deadly yellow fever common in tropical areas. Dr. Finlay had informed Major Walter Reed, president of the commission, that he believed the disease was carried and transmitted by a certain kind of mosquito. The commission has proved this to be true. The city of Havana has already begun a program aimed at wiping out mosquitoes. The commission advises people to drain away standing water, on which mosquitoes breed, and to cover still pools with oil. These methods should bring the terrible yellow fever epidemics in Cuba to an end.

Major Walter Reed, head of the U.S. Army Yellow Fever Commission.

NATIONS SEEK ASIAN ALLIES

Jan. 30, Washington The major countries of the world are eager to extend their power. They make friends with smaller countries, and often have naval or military bases there. These are their "spheres of influence."

The Japanese suggested that Manchuria should be Russia's "sphere of influence," while Korea should be Japan's. The Chinese have already allowed Russia to build the Trans-Siberian Railway across Manchuria to the Russian port of Vladivostok. The Russians have a naval base, Port Arthur, in southern Manchuria. But the czar does not want to give up all claim to Korea.

Now the Japanese have signed an agreement with Britain. It insures that Britain will not side with Russia in any future dispute.

CARIBBEAN TOWN VANISHES

May 8, Martinique A volcano, Mount Pelée, has erupted and wiped out the city of Saint-Pierre. A beautiful lake filling the crater was a favorite spot for French visitors. Last month people complained that there was a terrible smell of sulfur. Today about 38,000 people were overwhelmed by gas fumes and hot steam. Only three people survived. One, a shoemaker, described how he lay in his house, fighting for air. His legs were bleeding, and covered with burns. Another was locked in the only building left standing—the jail.

BOER WAR ENDS

June 1, Vereeniging, Transvaal, South Africa The South African War is over. The Boers have surrendered. Their food is short, many of their horses are dead, and they are exhausted. African tribes have raided their cattle. At midnight last night British and Boer leaders signed a peace treaty. The two Boer republics, the Transvaal, where the new gold mines are, and the Orange Free State, will become British. South Africa is now part of the British Empire.

The news was greeted with great joy by British soldiers, who can now return home. They cheered and fired their guns in salute. The Boer fighters will have to search the camps for their wives and children. Then they will try to rebuild their homes and their lives.

CELEBRATED AUTHOR DIES

Sept. 29, Paris The writer Emile Zola died today from carbon monoxide poisoning. The gas came from a charcoal stove in his bedroom. Emile Zola wrote novels about ordinary men and women. Once he spent six months among coal miners so as to write about them truthfully. His novel *The Drunkard* is about the misery of being poor. He was an outspoken socialist. Four years ago he accused a military court of convicting the wrong man in the trial of an army officer, Alfred Dreyfus. The article he wrote caused a scandal, and for a short time he had to leave France.

MINERS' STRIKE ENDS TODAY

Oct. 23, Washington The five-month-old strike in the hard-coal fields of Pennsylvania has led to a shortage of fuel in the United States. President Roosevelt has now reached a settlement with the miners' leader, John Mitchell, and the mine owners. Miners' wages will be increased and their working time reduced to nine hours a day. The 150,000 miners were ready to return to work. Without wages their families were starving, and winter is coming.

The union membership certificate of the United Mine Workers of America.

WILLIAMSBURG BRIDGE BURNS

Nov. 17, New York A dramatic fire blazed across part of the as yet unfinished Williamsburg Bridge over the East River yesterday. The flames spread from a work station to the bridge's wooden pedestrian walkway. Sparks flew 100 yards down to the river bank. Fireboats raced to the scene and houses in the area were evacuated. Crowds gathered to watch the fire burn itself out. Early reports say that four bridge workers are missing.

Fire-damaged Williamsburg Bridge.

NEWS IN BRIEF . . .

CHINESE END CRIPPLING CUSTOM

Feb. 1, Peking For a thousand years the Chinese have deformed their girl children's feet. They grow up hardly able to walk, with their toes bent under their feet by tight bandaging. In the old days, it was rich women who had to suffer in this way. It showed they did not have to work. Then the villagers copied the fashion. It made their hard compulsory farmwork extremely painful to perform. Now at last the emperor has said that this barbaric practice must end.

CHILDREN'S BOOKS SELLING WELL

Oct. 2, London Beatrix Potter has just published *The Tale of Peter Rabbit*. Young Peter, unlike his brothers and sisters, has one aim—to eat the lettuces in Mr. McGregor's garden. Mrs. Potter illustrates the story with delicate watercolors. The publishers have already sold 8,000 copies.

FASHIONS FLATTER THE FEMALE FIGURE

Aug. 1, Paris This year's fashions are ultra-feminine. Dressmakers and embroiderers are kept busy making up dresses, underslips, petticoats, blouses, skirts, collars, and cuffs. Most dresses or blouses have a boned collar that rises to the ears. Tightly laced corsets pull in the waist—to 18 inches (46 cm) for some young women!

Ladies of fashion change their clothes, with the help of a maid, at least three times a day. When they visit friends for a weekend house party, they naturally take their maids with them.

Fashionable ladies' elaborate evening gowns.

IT HAPPENED JUST SO

Dec. 1, South Africa Rudyard Kipling this year has written *Just So Stories*, fantasy tales about how things came about. They have titles such as "The Elephant's Child" and "How the Camel got its Hump." They follow *Kim*, a book about a young boy's adventures in India, where Kipling was born. He is now in Africa reporting the Boer War.

DAM HARNESSES NILE

Dec. 10, Cairo, Egypt As the sluice gates were opened today, a rush of water raced down the Nile River toward Cairo. The huge Aswan Dam, 590 miles (944 km) from the sea, is going to change Egyptian agriculture. In the past an annual flooding has watered the crops. Now the dam will let water through from the lake above it all the year round.

European and Egyptian guests cross the dam before its opening.

1903

ARTIST PAUL GAUGUIN DIES IN POLYNESIA

May 8, Marquesas Islands The painter Paul Gaugin, a Frenchman, has died at 55 on one of the tropical islands he loved. Once a successful banker, he turned to art as a career when the banking business crashed in 1883. He had already been painting and collecting art for 10 years. He had also met other French artists and was a friend of Dutch artist Vincent van Gogh. However, the experience that most persuaded him to devote his life to art was a visit to the island of Martinique in 1887. He was inspired by its brilliant colors and the simple life of its native people.

INTERNATIONAL RACE CANCELLED

May 26, Bordeaux, France The long awaited auto race from Paris to Madrid in Spain has been called off halfway through. Accidents happened when spectators unused to high speeds—up to 65 mph (104 kph)—wandered onto the road. Six were killed and many more injured.

PULITZER GIVES $2 MILLION FOR SCHOOL

Aug. 15, New York Joseph Pulitzer, publisher of *The World*, the nation's largest daily newspaper, has made a gift of $2 million to Columbia University. It is to be used to found a school of journalism that will provide training in the profession. Up to the present, newspaper writers—"the informers and teachers of the people," according to *The World*—have not had formal training such as that available to other professions.

Pulitzer himself is known as one of the founders of "yellow journalism." This is the kind of sensational reporting that deals largely with disasters, crimes, and scandals.

BOSTON WINS FIRST WORLD SERIES

Oct. 13, Boston The first inter-league series for the world baseball championship has been played out here. Today the Bostons of the American League triumphed over Pittsburgh of the National League 3-0. It was the eighth and last game of the series. Two home runs by a Boston player in the second game proved to be a turning point. Boston won five games to Pittsburgh's three. Cy Young pitched two of Boston's winning games. Honus Wagner got six hits for Pittsburgh. The well-established National League had been expected to win the series. The newer and less-respected American League has become famous.

Over 200 cars and 59 motorcycles took part in the Paris to Madrid race. This is the first car to reach Bordeaux—in 5 hours, 33 minutes.

HEAVIER-THAN-AIR MACHINE TAKES OFF

Dec. 17, Kitty Hawk, N.C. The Wright brothers, Orville and Wilbur, have proved that man can fly a heavier-than-air machine. Unlike a lighter-than-air balloon, their machine has wings. Today Orville Wright flew their homemade machine, the *Flyer*, for 59 whole seconds—almost a minute! The 12-horsepower (9-kilowatt) gasoline engine drives two wooden propellers with the aid of toughened bicycle chains. There are two wings, and Mr. Wright lay in the middle of the lower wing in a kind of cradle. He controlled the wings and the tail by moving his feet and hands.

The wings measure 40 feet 4 inches (12.3 m) long and are covered with cotton cloth. The propellers are fastened behind the wings. The *Flyer* does not have wheels. It has wooden runners instead.

The *Flyer* ended its flight in a nose-first plunge. But it seems that great things are on the way!

At Kitty Hawk in North Carolina, the Wright brothers, Orville and Wilbur, fly their machine for the first time.

NEW MOTION PICTURE IS HIT

Dec. 10, Chicago A new moving picture has proved popular in vaudeville theaters, music halls, and amusement arcades across the country. It is called *The Great Train Robbery*, and for 11 exciting minutes it shows a train being robbed and the pursuit and capture of the bandits. Directed by Edwin S. Porter, it creates suspense by switching back and forth between scenes of the robbers escaping and the sheriff's posse racing after them. This was the first time a moving picture was not shot in sequence. Instead, all the scenes that took place in a particular setting were shot at the same time. Then later, the movie film was pieced together to tell the story.

PLIGHT OF WORKERS REVEALED

Sept. 30, New York Two sisters, Marie and Bessie Van Vorst, have spent the past few months dressed as poor working women. They found out what conditions are like in factories and "sweatshops." They saw small children of about 8 or 10 years old working for 25 cents a day. There are over a million workers under 16. Women doing piecework at home earn less than a dollar for 14 hours' work. Many are underfed and suffer from tuberculosis. Garment workers, mainly Polish women, are fortunate in having their own trade union.

SERBIAN KING MURDERED

June 12, Belgrade Army officers yesterday broke into the royal palace and murdered King Alexander and Queen Droga. The king was hated because of his one-man rule. He did away with the constitution in April and dismissed ten judges. Newspapers today, free from censorship at last, say the rebels "rendered a tremendous service." In Turkey, where newspapers have no freedom, the royal couple are said to have died of indigestion.

The late King Alexander of Serbia.

MOTORCAR MAKES CROSS-COUNTRY TRIP

Aug. 21, New York A Model F Packard rolled into Columbus Circle here today, having completed a cross-country road trip in 51 days of actual driving time. A large and enthusiastic crowd waited to greet the drivers. Tom Fetch of the Packard Company and M.C. Karrup, a journalist, started their journey in San Francisco and drove an average of 80 miles (128 km) per day. Although gasoline motorcars were introduced in 1896, and R.E. Olds built 425 of them in 1901, many of the people they met along the way had never seen one.

PANAMA IS INDEPENDENT STATE

Nov. 6, Washington Panama has revolted against rule from the South American state of Colombia. Cut off from Panama by jungle and high ground, the Colombians approached by sea to put down the revolt. They briefly bombarded Panama City, killing one man and one donkey. The United States is hoping to build a canal across the narrow neck of land that joins North and South America. The canal will run through Panama. Two days ago we landed marines at Colón on the coast, and the Colombians departed without a fight.

WOMAN SHARES NOBEL PRIZE

Dec. 10, Stockholm, Sweden Madame Marie Curie is the first woman ever to win a Nobel Prize. She has been given this honor jointly with her husband, Pierre, and Monsieur Henri Becquerel. The three scientists have all done original work in what Madame Curie has called "radioactivity." She has shown that a new substance, called radium, sends out heat without chemical change. Two other substances discovered by the Curies, uranium and thorium, are also "radioactive."

Marie Curie and her husband Pierre.

NEWS IN BRIEF . . .

BLIND GIRL'S STORY TOLD

Mar. 31, Boston *The Story of My Life*, by Miss Helen Keller, has become an instant success. Miss Keller became blind, deaf, and mute as a child, but despite this she enjoys life to the full. Anne Sullivan, who herself is partially blind, has been her friend and teacher since she was 7 years old.

Helen Keller (left) and her teacher.

CONTROVERSIAL ARTIST DIES

July 17, London The American-born painter James Whistler died today aged 70. The critics did not like his pictures; Whistler sued his chief critic, John Ruskin, for writing insulting remarks. He won the court case, but was awarded only a quarter of a British penny in damages. However, the publicity did him good. At an exhibition he wrote the critics' remarks under each picture. The public did not agree with the critics, and his work began to sell.

NEW POPE CROWNED

Aug. 9, Rome Pope Pius X was crowned today in St. Peter's Church, Rome. The elaborate and colorful ceremony, which lasted five hours, was watched by 70,000 people. The previous pope, Leo XIII, died three weeks ago aged 93.

BICYCLE RACE IS A TOUGH RIDE

July 19, Paris The first bicycle race, which its inventor, Henry Desgrange, calls the "Tour de France," has ended today. A 32-year-old chimney sweep, Maurice Garin, crossed the finish line after 94½ hours' actual bicycling time. The next competitor did not arrive till three hours later. The 2,485-mile (4,000-km) route took the cyclists right down to Marseilles and back to Paris. For 17 days they cycled. They signed in at ten different places and there was a time limit for each of these stages. Mr. Garin says he rode late into the night to reach his targets in time. Out of 60 starters, 21 riders finished.

Whistler's "Nocturne in blue and gold."

The new pope, Pius X, in Rome.

POWERED FLIGHT FAILS

Oct. 7, Washington Professor Samuel P. Langley is a well-known scientist and secretary of the Smithsonian Institution. He has long been interested in powered flight. Some time ago he built a full-size gasoline-powered flying machine, which he called an *aerodrome*. Today a navigator launched the craft from a houseboat on the Potomac River. Unfortunately it plunged into the water after 100 yards.

BRUTALITY PUNISHED IN NORTH GERMANY

Dec. 15, Rensburg, Germany An army lieutenant has written a book about conditions in the German Army. He says that in Prussian regiments soldiers are frequently beaten almost to death. Several soldiers have committed suicide after being punished. In August an officer was found guilty of 576 incidents of brutality and he will be imprisoned for two and a half years.

1904

CONFLICT IN FAR EAST
JAPAN AND RUSSIA ARE AT WAR

Feb. 10, Manchuria The Russians have been moving troops into Korea to defend it against Japan. Czar Nicholas II thought that Japan would not dare to go to war with his huge country. He was wrong. Two days ago, at midnight, the Japanese torpedoed Russian warships at their naval base in Port Arthur, Manchuria. Their warships are now surrounding the harbor, and they have declared war on Russia. Russia cannot afford to fight a war, particularly one so far from home. It will take time for more troops to arrive in Port Arthur because the one-track Trans-Siberian Railway is not completed. Meanwhile, well-equipped Japanese troops are landing in Korea.

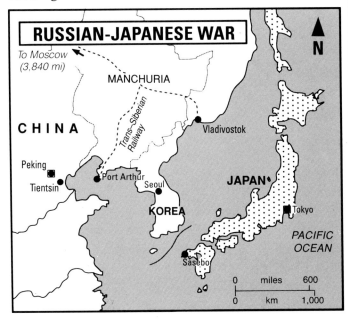

RUSSIAN-JAPANESE WAR

To Moscow (3,840 mi)

MANCHURIA

CHINA

Trans-Siberian Railway

Vladivostok

Peking

Port Arthur

Tientsin

Seoul

KOREA

JAPAN

Tokyo

PACIFIC OCEAN

Sasebo

0 miles 600
0 km 1,000

N

PORT ARTHUR IS BESIEGED

May 30, Manchuria The Japanese and Russians have fought a bitter battle near Port Arthur. The Russian General Anatoly Stössel ordered his troops to retreat. They are now besieged in Port Arthur by the Japanese land and sea forces.

RUSSIAN FLEET BADLY DAMAGED

Aug. 31, Manchuria The Russian flagship has limped into Port Arthur. It is badly damaged, and the fleet commander has been killed trying to lead his ships out of the harbor secretly. He was trying to make a dash for Vladivostok, but he encountered the Japanese Navy. Both sides tried to wreck the other's flagship. The Russian admiral and his officers were killed by shells, and the signaling equipment was destroyed. It took quite some time before the second-in-command, aboard another battleship, realized this. When he did, he signaled the fleet to retreat.

HORROR OF UNEXPLAINED SHELLING

Oct. 24, Hull, England Three days ago Russian warships shelled British fishing vessels off the Dogger Bank in the North Sea. One trawler was sunk and others badly damaged. The Russian fleet sailed on to Port Arthur without stopping. The Russian warships apparently thought the trawlers were Japanese warships. This incident has turned the British public against Russia. Ships of the Royal British Navy are sailing to the Dogger Bank to prevent further incidents.

ST. LOUIS EXPOSITION OPENS

April 30, St. Louis, Missouri The St. Louis World's Fair, officially known as the Louisiana Purchase Exposition, opened today to large crowds. The huge fair celebrates the area's 100th anniversary in the Union. Its themes are education and American know-how. The automobile will be one of the important exhibits, along with a newly invented treat called an ice-cream cone. Secretary of War William H. Taft, representing President Theodore Roosevelt, attended the opening ceremonies. So did officials from other states, territories, and countries. John Philip Sousa's band played to the delight of the crowd.

Varied Industries Building, St. Louis World's Fair.

EXPEDITION REACHES LHASA

Sept. 7, Lhasa, Tibet British and Tibetan representatives have signed a trade treaty. This is the end of a strange and sad story. The British viceroy in India thought the Russians were trying to control Tibet. He persuaded the British government to send out Colonel Francis Younghusband, the explorer, into Tibet to investigate. He took a thousand soldiers, Indian carriers, and pack animals.

On the way to Lhasa the army nearly froze to death, and many soldiers suffered from frostbite and snow blindness. When they arrived in Lhasa after eight months they found no sign of any Russians. The British troops had killed over 2,000 Tibetans; many of them were unarmed. The expedition's hardships were a high price to pay for an agreement to trade with Tibet.

STRANGE EVENTS AT OLYMPICS

Aug. 29, St. Louis, Missouri American competitors won most of the medals in this year's Olympics, held during the World's Fair here. The marathon attracted much attention. Fred Lorz of the United States arrived at the finishing post well ahead of the rest, and not at all out of breath. But he was disqualified. He admitted that he rode on a truck for part of the way!

FRENCH AGREE TO LEAVE EGYPT

April 8, Paris French people booed King Edward VII of Britain when he visited France last year. They now cheer him whenever he appears in public. Today an *entente cordiale*, or friendly understanding, was signed by French and British delegates. The French have agreed to leave Egypt, which they have been ruling jointly with Britain. In return they expect Britain to give them a mandate over Morocco if the sultan's rule should end.

The sultan has very little control over Morocco. Berber tribesmen have seized the capital, Fez. They are led by a man named Bu Hamara ("The Man with a Donkey"), who accuses the sultan of following Western ways.

Ships of the French fleet visit England.

SCOTT EXPLORES SOUTH

Nov. 7, London Tonight Captain Robert Falcon Scott spoke about his adventure as the first person to reach the South Polar plateau. For three years his ship *Discovery* has been home to scientists collecting information about the plants and animals of these barren lands. Captain Scott led explorers far out onto the ice toward the South Pole.

"SQUARE DEAL" PRESIDENT WINS

Nov. 9, Washington Theodore Roosevelt has been reelected President of the United States. His motto is "Speak softly and carry a big stick." This is how he hopes to conduct his foreign policy: courteously but firmly. His campaign supporters wore a badge that promised "A square deal for all."

Scott's ship *Discovery* abandoned in frozen Antarctic seas. From April to July each year the sun never rose above the horizon. When food ran out, the explorers lived on seal and dog meat.

NEWS IN BRIEF . . .

OUTDOOR SMOKING? MEN ONLY!

Sept. 28, New York Today a vigilant policeman arrested a young lady as she sat in an auto on New York's fashionable Fifth Avenue. What had she done? Nothing illegal; but she was smoking a cigarette in full view of people passing by. The tobacco industry, through advertising, encourages every adult to smoke cigarettes. But the police seem to think that ladies should smoke only in private.

NEW RODIN SCULPTURE

November, Paris Auguste Rodin, the famous French sculptor, has shown an important new work. The bronze figure is called "The Thinker." It has the great vitality and power of his finest works. However, it will probably not cause the controversy of his much-discussed 1898 sculpture, "The Kiss." This piece was refused admission to the Chicago World's Fair as "unfit for public exhibition."

Rodin began his career in 1877 with a bronze figure. It looked so real that some said it had been cast from a living person.

1905

RUSSIA'S ENEMIES AT HOME AND ABROAD

UNARMED WORKERS MASSACRED

Jan. 22, St. Petersburg Many hundreds of unarmed demonstrators, men, women, and children, were killed today and thousands more were wounded in the square outside the czar's Winter Palace. A young church leader Father George Gapon led a peaceful demonstration to protest to the czar about working conditions, and against the war with Japan. The people's message was "Destroy the wall between yourself and your people," for they believe that the czar is not told about working conditions by his ministers. They chanted "God save the czar." But the czar had fled. Police and soldiers were called out, and they fired into the crowd of about 200,000 people. Tonight the square is full of the dead and the injured.

RUSSIA LOSES BATTLE IN MANCHURIA

March 10, Manchuria Port Arthur fell to the Japanese in January. For the past two weeks the Russians have been hard pressed near the Manchurian town of Mukden. Each side has lost about 60,000 men. In spite of successful charges by the Cossacks, Russia's cavalry, the Russians have now had to give in to the nation they call "The Yellow Peril." The Russian general has resigned.

The Russians are now relying on their navy. A fleet of battleships left the Baltic Sea in November. They have to sail halfway around the world: west of Africa and across the Indian Ocean.

Troops attack the crowd of men, women, and children at the Winter Palace in St. Petersburg.

RUSSIAN FLEET DESTROYED

May 27, Japan Today Japanese warships caught the Russian fleet in the narrow waters between Japan and Korea, the Tsushima Strait. In a battle lasting 24 hours, Admiral Heihachiro Togo scored a great victory for Japan. His ships surrounded the Russian fleet and sunk or damaged most of its ships. Nearly 5,000 Russian sailors have been killed. It is the first time in history that an Asian country has defeated a European one.

RUSSIAN DISCONTENT OVER DEFEAT

June 27, St. Petersburg News of the disaster at Tsushima has reached the Russian capital. People are angry with the czar's handling of the war. The crew of the battleship *Potemkin* has mutinied, thrown the officers overboard, and sailed the ship to Odessa. Here sympathizers have been fighting in the streets, and several thousand people have been killed in the disturbances.

The Russian battleship *Potemkin*.

CZAR APPOINTS PRIME MINISTER

Oct. 17, St. Petersburg With two million people on strike and industry at a standstill, Czar Nicholas II has at last agreed that in the future he will not rule alone. He has appointed a parliament, the Duma, with a prime minister, Count Sergey Witte. Members of the new Socialist parties are afraid that the czar and his successors will still have too much power. His chief critic is a leader of the Workers' Soviet (council) in St. Petersburg, Leo Trotsky.

KAISER VISITS MOROCCO

March 31, Tangier Last year Britain agreed that France should have a mandate over Morocco. The Germans feel that they have been left out. The German kaiser has arrived on a visit to Morocco. He rode through the streets of this port on a magnificent Berber horse. He told the Moroccan sultan, Abdul Aziz, that all European nations should be equal trading partners with Morocco. The French are not likely to be pleased.

PETER PAN OPENS ON BROADWAY

Nov. 6, New York The charming actress Maude Adams opened tonight at the Empire Theater to enthusiastic reviews. She is appearing in the title role of playwright James Barrie's *Peter Pan*. This is a delightful fantasy about a magic boy who refuses to grow up and has run away to Never-Never Land to avoid adulthood. In the play he visits the human world and flies back to his home taking with him three human children for many exciting adventures.

Miss Adams first appeared on a stage at the age of six months! Her original appearance in New York was in 1892 when she was 20. But she became really famous in 1897 when she appeared in James Barrie's *The Little Minister*.

RUSSIANS AND GERMANS IN ALLIANCE

July 20, Baltic Sea The German kaiser today met the Russian czar on board a ship off the Baltic coast, and agreed on an alliance. After his country's defeat in Japan, the czar is happy to unite with a strong country. The desire for "spheres of influence" as countries take sides in international disputes could lead to war on a grand scale.

The czar (left) welcomes his new ally, the kaiser, aboard his yacht.

NEW RULES FOR FOOTBALL

Dec. 9, Philadelphia Members of the public have been very concerned about what they consider the "brutality" of football. Even President Theodore Roosevelt supports some reform of the rules that govern this popular game. In response, the Intercollegiate Rules Committee met here today. The members suggested certain new rules that would "render foul play unprofitable." They also urged that all football officials be made responsible to a single governing body. In this way, it is hoped that the rules might be applied consistently and the number of serious injuries reduced.

NEWS IN BRIEF . . .

JEWS MARK 250 YEARS IN AMERICA

Nov. 26, New York Special services were held in synagogues here and elsewhere in the United States today. They celebrated the 250th anniversary of the settlement of Jews in America. A group of Jews settled in New York as early as 1655. Jews also founded their synagogues in Philadelphia, Newport, R.I., Savannah, Ga., and Charleston, S.C. Some people believe that the first Jew to set foot on American soil was Louis de Torres, who they say was with Columbus's expedition in 1492.

JOHN HAY DEAD AT 66

July 1, Sunapee, N.H. Secretary of State John Milton Hay died here today. Born in Salem, Ind., Hay had a long career in public life. As a young man he served as private secretary to President Abraham Lincoln. In 1897 President William McKinley named Hay our ambassador to Britain. The following year he became secretary of state. Hay may be best remembered for his support of what he called an "Open-Door Policy" toward China. He wanted all nations to have an equal right to trade in China. He also tried to persuade some of the more powerful countries to allow weaker China its independence.

THE GREAT MAN IS ALIVE

March 31, London Sherlock Holmes is back! In the last story about the great detective, he and his deadly enemy, Professor Moriarity, disappeared over a cliff in Switzerland. His inventor, Sir Arthur Conan Doyle, was tired of him! But now, by popular demand, he and Dr. Watson are detecting again, in *The Return of Sherlock Holmes*.

Holmes stories are printed in the *Strand Magazine*. The magazine does not print serial stories, so Sir Arthur decided to write a series of different adventures. This had not been tried before. People love them so much that they think of Sherlock Holmes as a real person.

1906

PRESIDENT'S DAUGHTER MARRIES

Feb. 17, Washington Alice Lee Roosevelt, the elder daughter of President Theodore Roosevelt, was married in the White House today. The bridegroom is Nicholas Longworth, a congressman from Ohio and the speaker of the House of Representatives. The whole country has been following ''Princess Alice's'' romance with great interest. The ceremony took place in the East Room and was conducted by Henry Y. Saterlee, the bishop of Washington.

Mrs. Longworth wore a princess-style gown of white satin trimmed with lace. Silver brocade satin made up the train. She also wore a long veil attached to a crown of orange blossoms. She held a bouquet of orchids.

NEW TUNNEL THROUGH ALPS

May 19, Iselle, Italy A railroad tunnel that cuts through the Swiss Alps and links Switzerland with Italy opened today. King Victor Emmanuel of Italy officiated at the opening. An engineering wonder, the Simplon Tunnel is the longest in the world. It starts at Brig, Switzerland in the Rhône Valley and ends 12 miles (20 km) away at Iselle. At its highest point it is 2,300 feet (705 m). The project started about 100 years ago when Napoleon built a military road over the Simplon Pass.

AFRICAN UPRISING PUT DOWN

Feb. 27, Songea, Tanganyika Africans in this German colony are rebelling against foreign rule. This rebellion is called the Maji Maji Uprising. A ''prophet'' named Kinjikitile supplied people with *maji* (medicine) that he said would turn European bullets to water. Hundreds of Africans stormed a government outpost, where they were killed by machine guns. A shocked African said: ''They were severely beaten as the machine guns helped the Germans very much. They fought up to five in the evening. When they realized they were being killed in numbers, they fled, crying, 'Kinjikitile, you have cheated us.''' Similar incidents occurred all over the country. The situation is now under control. Some African leaders have been hanged.

Africans work long hours on European plantations, cultivating crops for export. They have little time to tend their own fields, on which they depend for their food. As in other European-owned African countries, the Africans here have no say in the government.

VIOLENT EARTH SHOCKS CAUSE DAMAGE

FAMOUS VOLCANO ERUPTS

April 8, Naples, Italy The top of Mount Vesuvius in southern Italy has been blown off by a violent eruption. Onlookers saw a huge cloud "like a pine tree." There were vivid lightning flashes as lava poured down the mountainside. A town has been destroyed, villages are half buried, and 105 people died when a church roof collapsed.

EARTHQUAKE NEARLY DESTROYS CITY

April 19, San Francisco Yesterday a tremendous earthquake severely damaged this California city. Starting at dawn, a series of shocks tore up roads and split buildings. Fires, caused by broken gas mains, have destroyed more property than the earthquake itself. Firemen were powerless, as the town's water mains were out of action. Thieves trying to loot shops have been shot by police and soldiers. It is one of the worst earthquakes ever recorded. Almost a thousand people have died, and about 250,000 have been left homeless.

Sacramento Street in San Francisco after the earthquake devastated the city.

NEW QUAKE IN SOUTH AMERICA

Aug. 18, Chile Valparaiso and Santiago have been partially destroyed by an earthquake that has left thousands dead. About 40 villages and towns also suffered heavy damage. The earthquake followed a night of pouring rain.

TYPHOON STRIKES HONG KONG

Sept. 18, Hong Kong Winds and heavy rain raged here today for two hours. Large ships were driven onto the shore, and hundreds of fishing boats were sunk. There are 10,000 people dead or missing in this area on the southern coast of China.

MOROCCO TO BE FRENCH MANDATE

March 31, Algeciras, Spain An international conference on North Africa has just ended. The delegates finally agreed that France should have a mandate over Morocco. This means that France will protect the country, and have certain trading rights there. The sultan will still rule the country, under Muslim laws. Spain holds some ports and the southwestern part of the country.

France now has a great bloc of west and northwest Africa under its control. European nations have successfully partitioned Africa among them. Only Ethiopia and Liberia remain truly independent.

TICKS CAUSE DISEASE

June 4, Chicago Rocky Mountain spotted fever is a dangerous and often fatal disease. Its effects are somewhat like those of typhus, starting with chills and fever and pains in muscles and joints. Later a rash appears. The cause of this severe illness has long been unknown. Now, however, Howard Taylor Ricketts, a scientist and professor at the University of Chicago, has discovered that it is transmitted by the bite of certain ticks. Ticks are related to spiders and mites. Having discovered the cause, there is now hope that further discoveries may lead to some treatment and control of this dangerous disease.

NEWS IN BRIEF . . .

TRAPPED MINERS RESCUED

March 30, Courrières, France After 20 long days underground, 13 coal miners have been brought to the surface alive. A huge explosion at daybreak on March 10 wrecked the hoists that carry miners underground. Altogether, 1,800 miners were either in the hoists or already underground, and 1,787 died.

Government officials at the mine.

PRESIDENT HONORED

Dec. 10, Stockholm, Sweden President Roosevelt has won the Nobel Peace Prize because he had persuaded Russia and Japan to end their war. The peace treaty was signed in September at Portsmouth, New Hampshire. Roosevelt is the first American to be honored in this way.

Dreyfus receives the Legion of Honor.

ANTI-JEWISH RIOTS

June 15, St. Petersburg The Russian legislative assembly was asked today whether it is trying to stop offenses against Jews. Yesterday peasant mobs attacked a Jewish quarter and killed several hundred people. The peasants claimed that the Jews fired on a religious procession and two priests and several children were killed. The police took the side of the peasants, and distributed leaflets saying Jews should be wiped out.

ARMY OFFICER HONORED

July 21, Paris Everyone in France has heard of the Jewish army officer Major Alfred Dreyfus, and taken sides for or against him. In 1895 he denied spying for Germany. But he was found guilty and imprisoned on Devil's Island, in French Guiana.

Major Dreyfus was pardoned six years ago, but his innocence was not proved. Since then the real culprit has been found. Today Major Dreyfus was enrolled in the Legion of Honor.

1907

CONGO CHANGES HANDS

AFRICANS' SUFFERING REVEALED

May 1, Washington Shocking reports are being received from the Congo Free State. This country in west-central Africa was established by King Leopold II of Belgium in 1885. He still personally owns this territory, which is 80 times the size of Belgium. He has become rich from the sale of its wild rubber and ivory. The Africans must pay taxes to Belgium. As they have no currency, they pay not in money, but in wild rubber. To get enough rubber, they work long hours, deep in the forests. If they do not collect enough, they are punished. Some are brutally beaten, others have their hands cut off. Protests are mounting both here and in Great Britain against the cruelty of Leopold's agents toward the Africans.

CONGO CONDITIONS WORSEN

July 29, Washington More appalling news has been heard about conditions in the Congo Free State. It was reported that the population there has fallen by three million in only 15 years. Much of this is due to a terrible epidemic of sleeping sickness, the disease caused by the bite of the tsetse fly. Survivors are too weak to harvest the wild rubber. Thousands of villagers have died from exhaustion, starvation, or disease. Thousands more have been shot. The elephant herds have dwindled. The wild rubber trees have all been tapped, and nobody has planted any more.

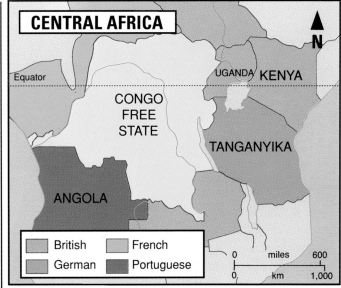

BELGIAN GOVERNMENT BUYS CONGO

Nov. 28, Brussels The Belgian government is going to buy the Congo Free State from the king. This has been decided after much debate in the Belgian parliament. The Belgian people did not know that the king's agents were mistreating the Africans and managing the country so badly.

SOUTH AFRICAN RACE LAW RESISTED

March 22, Pretoria A new law in the Transvaal state of South Africa has angered Indians. In the future they will be fingerprinted, and will have to carry identity cards. Their leader, Mohandas Gandhi, is calling for people to resist the new law by peaceful means. Mr. Gandhi was born in northwestern India. He trained as a lawyer in England, and has been a lawyer in South Africa for 14 years.

GERMAN SPEED RECORD BROKEN

Oct. 11, Sandy Hook, N.J. The British liner *Lusitania* sailed into New York Harbor today. It had just succeeded in breaking the transatlantic crossing speed record that was previously held by the German-owned *Deutschland* by several hours. Carrying 1,200 passengers and 650 crew members, it made the trip from Ireland, in four days, 19 hours, and 52 minutes. The luxury liner averaged a little over 24 knots. The British hope this record can also be bettered. New developments in turbine engines have produced speeds as high as 35 knots. Naturally, passengers on this record-breaking trip expressed themselves as thrilled at having been part of an exciting experience.

WORKERS WAGE WINE WAR

June 20, Narbonne, France Police fired on demonstrators today as the "wine war" enters its second month. Wine growers are protesting low prices. Although Prime Minister Georges Clemenceau backs social reform, he deals harshly with strikers. Last month he called in the troops when strikers burned the town hall and police station in another wine-growing town.

Vineyard workers riot in the Champagne district.

"WOBBLIES" LEADER ACQUITTED OF MURDER

July 28, Boise, Idaho Clarence Darrow, the brilliant defense lawyer, has been defending labor leader "Big Bill" Haywood in a murder trial. When Frank Steunenberg, former governor of Idaho, was killed by a bomb, Haywood and his colleague, Harry Orchard, were arrested. Orchard has admitted that he planted the bomb. There is no evidence against Haywood, though he is known to favor violence. He helped found the Industrial Workers of the World (known as the Wobblies) two years ago. Their aim is to overthrow capitalism. Darrow has persuaded the jury to acquit Haywood.

PUBLIC WITHDRAWS MONEY FROM BANKS

Nov. 4, New York Businessmen in the United States all invest in stocks and shares. There are even special share offices for ladies. The economy has been booming for ten years. Recently an investor's gamble on the Stock Exchange failed, and the bank backing him lost heavily. Bank customers were afraid that the bank would collapse, and rushed to take out their money. Soon customers were closing their accounts with other banks. Fortunately during this panic, John Pierpont Morgan, leading financier and head of U.S. Steel Corporation, loaned money to the banks. This kept them from being forced to close.

NEWS IN BRIEF . . .

PLAZA HOTEL OPENS

Oct. 1, New York Described as the most beautiful hotel in the world, the Plaza opened here last night. A gala, celebrity-attended dinner marked the occasion. It was held in a small banquet hall on the main floor. The room was brilliantly lighted by numerous electric chandeliers. It was decorated by sparkling mirrors lavishly draped with rose-colored satin. This room is thought by many to be the most beautiful in the city.

TAXI! TAXI!

May 31, New York The first taxicabs to run on meters — 65 of them — have been seen in New York streets. The bright red motors have been imported from France. Policemen now have new duties, to direct traffic in busy towns.

ARTIST PAINTED IN NEW STYLE

Oct. 15, Paris An exhibition of 60 paintings by the French artist Paul Cézanne here in Paris is revealing the artist's remarkable control of blocks of color. He sees the shapes of nature in terms of cylinders, spheres, and squares. He seems to have changed the art of painting — a change which the Spanish artist Pablo Picasso is continuing. Cézanne was still hard at work painting when he died last year.

GREAT WHITE FLEET SAILS

Oct. 31, Japan President Roosevelt has sent a fleet of 16 new battleships to sail around the world. They are painted white. This "goodwill cruise" is also meant to show the strength of America's navy. The President was not sure if the fleet would be welcome in Japan. Japanese immigration into the United States has recently been restricted. It follows a quarrel that broke out when San Francisco set up separate schools for Asian children. This has now been altered.

Though many Japanese who wished to emigrate to America are dismayed, Japan gave the American sailors a great welcome. On its return, the fleet will have sailed 46,000 miles.

SUFFRAGETTES RALLY

Dec. 31, New York American women do not have the right to vote. "Suffragettes" are women who work toward obtaining this right. Today a group of suffragettes held a rally in Madison Square. Their leaders spoke to an audience composed mainly of men. They said that allowing women to vote could only improve conditions in the U.S. Then they asked people to sign a petition urging Congress to give women the vote.

WARTIME NURSE HONORED

Nov. 29, London Miss Florence Nightingale has been granted the British Order of Merit by the king. She is the first woman to receive this honor. Only 24 people are entitled to put "OM" after their names at any one time.

During the Crimean War, in 1854, Miss Nightingale ran a hospital for wounded soldiers in Russia. She raised the standard of care so that far fewer men died. Thousands owe their lives to the nurse they called "the Lady with the Lamp."

Florence Nightingale, center, was honored today with the Order of Merit.

1908

TURKISH PARTY OPPOSES SULTAN

TURKISH GENERAL ASSASSINATED

July 7, Monastir, Macedonia A Turkish general has today been shot dead in the streets of Monastir. He was sent by the sultan of Turkey, Abdul Hamid II, to put down a mutiny in the Turkish Army. The rebellious soldiers have joined the "Young Turk" movement. The Young Turks are not necessarily young, but belong to a political party of this name that opposes the sultan. The party believes he is ruining their country, which was once the center of the great Ottoman Empire.

Last month the British king and the Russian czar discussed self-rule for Macedonia, which is a Turkish possession. The Young Turks are afraid the sultan will agree to give up Macedonia. The Turkish Empire has already lost many of its former colonies because of the sultan's weakness.

SULTAN MUST APPOINT PARLIAMENT

July 24, Constantinople After pressure from the Young Turks, the sultan has agreed that Turkey should have a constitution and a parliament. Even the words "constitution" and "parliament" have been banned from newspapers for many years for fear of what the ordinary people would demand. The sultan has always opposed change. The Young Turks hope that free discussion in a parliament will help Turkey develop new ideas, and take its place in the world as a modern nation, rather than as a country always looking to the past.

ANCIENT PALACE IS FOUND

Aug. 27, Crete The archaeologist Sir Arthur Evans is excavating a huge forgotten palace on the island of Crete. He has found hundreds of stone tablets, all with unreadable characters in Greek script. They are 3,000 years old. A remarkable wall painting shows a girl acrobat leaping over a bull. Thousands of years ago the Greek poet Homer wrote: "there is Knossos, the great city, the place where Minos was king." Sir Arthur believes he has found Knossos, King Minos's capital city. He is calling this ancient civilization "Minoan."

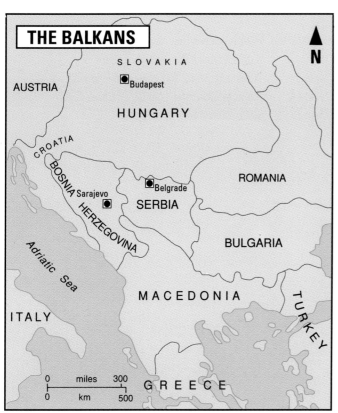

THE BALKANS

SLOVAKIA

AUSTRIA

Budapest

HUNGARY

CROATIA

BOSNIA

Sarajevo

HERZEGOVINA

Belgrade

SERBIA

ROMANIA

Adriatic Sea

MACEDONIA

BULGARIA

ITALY

TURKEY

GREECE

0 miles 300
0 km 500

N

FORD PRODUCES FIRST MODEL T

Aug. 12, Detroit Henry Ford, head of the Ford Motor Company, has long wanted to make an automobile that not just the rich could afford. Today he produced his first Model T. It seats two and sells for $850. It is not fancy, but it is sturdy and easy to drive. Ford feels it is still too expensive for many and hopes to introduce new production systems that will cut the cost still further.

ARMS RACE FOR WAR?

Aug. 11, Germany King Edward VII of Britain has met his nephew, Kaiser Wilhelm II of Germany, to talk about their "spheres of influence." The two men do not get along very well, but everyone hopes they can agree. The arms race is alarming. The navies of both countries are building more and more battleships. The Germans count on their zeppelins to control the skies.

Wilhelm II, the German kaiser.

CRISIS IN THE BALKANS

Oct. 6, Belgrade, Serbia Two surprise moves have angered the Serbians and alerted western nations. Yesterday Bulgaria proclaimed its independence from the Turkish Empire, and today the Austrians took Bosnia Herzegovina, also from the Turks.

Serbia has always wanted to join up with Bosnia, once a Serbian territory. The Serbians are now talking of war with Austria, which has the support of Germany. Once again European nations are taking sides and forming alliances.

ROOSEVELT FORMS CONSERVATION COMMISSION

June 8, Washington President Roosevelt has always been concerned about preserving our forests and wildlife. He has set aside millions of acres to be protected in national parks and forests. Now he is shocked by the excessive felling of trees and the shooting of rare birds and animals and even the stealing of rocks and minerals. Today, President Roosevelt has called for a National Conservation Commission to make the first official inventory of our country's natural resources.

TAFT ELECTED PRESIDENT

Nov. 3, Washington Former Secretary of War William Howard Taft was elected President today, defeating Democrat William Jennings Bryan. President Roosevelt had decided not to seek reelection this year, and Taft was his choice to succeed him in office. At first Mr. Taft was reluctant to run, but was persuaded to do so.

CHINESE EMPRESS DOWAGER DIES

Nov. 14, Peking Empress Dowager T'zu-hsi (Cixi) died today. Because of her ambition, treachery, and cruelty, there are persistent rumors that she was murdered. T'zu-hsi was the effective ruler of China between 1862 and her death. However, her control of the imperial court began as early as 1851. She was so powerful that she managed to defeat all attempts by China at democratic change and modernization. In fact, she had officials who were in favor of change executed.

BIG CROWD AT FIFTH OLYMPICS

Oct. 31, White City, London A huge new stadium was built at White City for the Olympic Games. In spite of bad weather, a large crowd turned out to see 21 different sports, including rowing (at Henley) and tennis (at Wimbledon). Three American runners seemed to block the way for a British runner in the 400 meters. Americans refused a rerun, so the British runner was given an unexpected win.

The marathon winner was disqualified for being helped over the line! He was given an unofficial prize.

SICILIAN TOWN DESTROYED

Dec. 29, Messina, Italy The worst earthquake ever recorded in Europe, and a huge tidal wave, yesterday hit Messina, a port on the east coast of Sicily. It is estimated that 84,000 people died here, and across the straits on the "toe" of Italy. The Sicilian shoreline sank by about 20 inches overnight. Most of the houses and shops, the 900-year-old Norman cathedral, and many beautiful churches have been totally destroyed.

The port of Messina in ruins and in flames after the earthquake.

NEWS IN BRIEF . . .

PROTEST LEADER JAILED

Jan. 10, Pretoria, South Africa The leader of the Indian community here, Mohandas Gandhi, has been jailed for two months. Thousands of Indians have left the province because they refuse to carry identity cards. Many are traders, and their absence is hurting South Africa's economy.

AIRSHIP TOTALLY DESTROYED

Aug. 5, Germany A zeppelin went up in flames today after it had been hit by lightning. Several passengers were injured. The airship was on the ground at the time, refueling its 16 gas tanks with hydrogen. It was returning after a test flight to Lake Constance, where it is moored.

TRAIN RUNS UNDER RIVER

Feb. 15, New York Railroad service under the Hudson River between New York and New Jersey began today. President Theodore Roosevelt turned on the electric power for the line by pressing a button in the White House. On this first day, 100,000 passengers made the trip in only 10.5 minutes—three times faster than the ferry ride across the river.

PROFESSOR WINS NOBEL PRIZE

Dec. 10, Stocklohm, Sweden The Nobel Prize for chemistry has been won by Professor Ernest Rutherford. He won for his new "theory of atomic transmutation": An atom gives off electrically charged particles called alpha and beta rays. This process changes the atom to a different chemical form. In effect, it becomes a new atom.

CHINA'S NEW RULER ENTHRONED

Dec. 2, Peking Pu yi has become emperor of China. He will be three years old in February. The Empress T'zu-hsi died suddenly and mysteriously last month, a day after the unexpected death of her nephew, the emperor.

Ernest Rutherford in his laboratory

1909

FREUD TO LECTURE IN U.S.

Jan. 10, Worcester, Mass. Austrian physician Sigmund Freud has become well known in the treatment of mental illnesses. His fame has spread to the U.S. and he has been invited to lecture at Clark University here this year.

Freud has devised the term "psychoanalysis" for his new method of treating mental illness. His theories and treatment are the cause of much discussion and argument. Freud believes that his patients' symptoms have to do with disturbing experiences they had early in life. He helps them uncover these hidden experiences by interpreting their dreams and by hypnotizing them. He also helps his patients recognize forgotten thoughts and actions through a system called "free association."

NEW SKYSCRAPER COMPLETED

Jan. 29, New York The largest office building in the world was completed here today. It is 50 stories tall and has four huge outdoor clocks at the level of the 25th floor. Each number on the clocks is four feet high and each hand weighs 1,000 pounds. Owned by the Metropolitan Life Insurance Company, it is located at 24th St. and Madison Ave. New York also boasts the 21-floor Flatiron Building, completed in 1903.

New York City now has almost as many skyscrapers as Chicago. Chicago started building these giants in 1890 with the Rand McNally Building. However, the Metro Tower proves that a skyscraper can be beautiful as well as big. It was patterned after the Campanile of Saint Mark's Church in Venice, Italy.

BELGIUM HAS NEW KING

Dec. 23, Brussels Today Prince Albert succeeded Leopold II as king of Belgium. Thousands turned out at dawn to cheer him along the route of the royal procession. People seemed happy at the prospect of a new era. For most of his reign the old king was condemned for his brutal treatment of the Congo Free State, now the Belgian Congo. Prince Albert promised fair treatment of that area.

FRENCHMAN FLIES CHANNEL

July 25, Dover, England Monsieur Louis Blériot has become the first person to fly across the English Channel. He landed his 25 horsepower monoplane on the white cliffs of Dover in a high wind. He flew the 23 miles (37 km) in under 40 minutes, an average of 40 mph (64 kph). He was shown a good landing place by two men waving red flags. M. Blériot wins a large cash prize.

TRAGIC EVENTS SHOCK SPAIN

RIOTING IN BARCELONA ALARMS GOVERNMENT

July 27, Barcelona Disturbances in this Spanish port have alarmed the king and the government. Last week women demonstrated in Madrid. Their sons and husbands had been drafted because of a crisis in Spanish Morocco. The women lay across the railroad lines in front of the trains. Soldiers' pay is very low, and the women were afraid they would be left at home to starve.

The socialists have called a general strike, hoping that all workers in Spain will stop work. Trains taking soldiers to the troopships have been halted. Any streetcars that were still running have been overturned in the streets.

CHURCH SEEN AS "THE ENEMY"

Aug. 1, Barcelona This week is being called "Tragic Week." The cause of the riots has shifted from the draft to the Church. Workers blame Church leaders for their poor education, which leads to a life of poverty. They live in overcrowded apartments, on wages which are barely enough to keep them alive. They believe the Spanish Catholic Church is rich, and they have burned 50 religious buildings, and turned the monks and nuns out into the street. The government is particularly shocked because the rioters mocked the Church by dressing up in the priests' clothing.

ALLEGED LEADER EXECUTED

Oct. 13, Barcelona Spanish workers are bewildered by the news that the wealthy Francisco Ferrer has been executed. Señor Ferrer set up a number of good independent schools, which the local bishop openly condemned. The government claims that Ferrer was responsible for the summer riots, although he was in England at the time. The workers deny they had a leader. It seems that the government is trying to restore order through fear.

PEARY REACHES NORTH POLE

Dec. 21, New York The National Geographical Society has awarded a gold medal to Commander Robert Peary. On April 6, Commander Peary, with a Negro American named Matthew Henson and four Eskimo guides, reached the North Pole. They traveled 800 miles (1,300 km) on moving ice fields. Another explorer, Mr. Frederick Cook, claims to have reached the North Pole first, exactly a year earlier. Experts have investigated, and believe Commander Peary. They think that Mr. Cook's claim is a hoax.

"I have got the North Pole out of my system after twenty-three years of effort, hard work, disappointments, hardships, privations, more or less suffering, and some risks. I have won the last great geographical prize of the North Pole for the credit of the United States."

Robert Peary, 1910

SERBIA SETTLES FOR PEACE

March 31, Belgrade Last year Austria took Bosnia-Herzegovina from the Turkish Empire. Serbia, which is a neighbor of Bosnia-Herzegovina, drafted men into the army and prepared to go to war with Austria. In return, Austria refused to renew an important trade agreement with the Serbians unless they disarmed. The Austrians were ready to invade Serbia at that time.

Britain and France urged Serbia to give in. Reluctantly, Serbia has now agreed "to live in future on good neighborly terms" with the Austrian Empire, and conflict was avoided.

In the Balkans, political boundaries do not follow those of national communities. There are Serbians in Bosnia, Romanians in Serbia, Bosnians in Croatia, and so on. This is bound to lead to unrest. There are rivalries between the different communities over trade, political power, and natural resources.

AMERICANS SPEAK MANY LANGUAGES

Nov. 13, Washington The population of the United States has now reached 92 million. Over a million immigrants have been arriving every year in recent times. They come mainly from Italy, Britain, the Austrian Empire, and Russia. New York has the largest number of Jewish people in any city of the world. Thousands of them escaped from persecution in Russia three years ago.

But the new life in America is not so easy. Some immigrants cannot speak English. They stay with others from the same country, often crowded together in poor slum housing. The more ambitious ones set to work to learn English so that they can look for well-paid jobs. Canada, Argentina, Australia, and South Africa also welcome immigrants, as they have a shortage of labor.

People seem to be on the move all over the world. Whole families are buying cheap steamer tickets and taking a passage to "a better land."

NEWS IN BRIEF . . .

WOMEN'S WEAR IS SHORTER

Aug. 1, Paris "If you wish to see old-fashioned clothes kindly continue to frequent English (fashion) houses." So says Paris dress designer Poiret. No boned collars or sweeping trains for him! He has even done away with the tight corset. His dresses hang straight from the shoulders, and often stop above the ankle. Poiret prefers strong colors, set off by jewels and perhaps a feather or two. For playing golf many ladies wear turn-down collars and ties and tweed caps.

Schoolgirls wear short skirts, blouses, black stockings, and ankle-strap shoes. They grow their hair long and tie it back off the forehead.

Dresses from M. Poiret's collection.

TURKEY TO HAVE NEW SULTAN

April 22, Constantinople Sultan Abdul Hamid has been deposed. He was allowed to leave by the Young Turks, who are the majority party in the new government. Officials entered his palace and removed his treasure from locked rooms. The deposed sultan's brother is now ruling as Muhammad V.

JOAN OF ARC IS "BLESSED"

April 18, Rome The French have a feast day to honor Joan of Arc who was burned at the stake by the English in 1431. Joan, a peasant girl, led 6,000 soldiers against the English, who were trying to seize France. She was only 19 when she died. Today Pope Pius X has declared that she is "blessed." This means that one day the Catholic Church will make her a saint.

PEOPLE OF 1900-1909

Theodore Roosevelt (1858-1919)

Theodore ("Teddy") Roosevelt was an astute politician. He became Vice-President in 1900, and a year later he was sworn in as President, after President William McKinley was assassinated.

Roosevelt became well known as a "trust buster." During his presidency many huge trusts, or business monopolies, were broken up in the hope of increasing competition and lowering prices. He arranged a treaty that led to the building of the Panama Canal. He was interested in conservation, and undertook to provide irrigation for the drier western states. He was also a sportsman and he loved big game hunting.

He was the first American to receive the Nobel Peace Prize: this was for negotiating the end of the Russo-Japanese War in 1904.

Wilbur and Orville Wright (1867-1912 and 1871-1948)

From a very early age these two American aviation pioneers were interested in mechanics. The brothers made their own mechanical toys as children. In their twenties they began to make and sell bicycles, which had become very popular.

About 1896 they became seriously interested in flying and flying machines. They built model gliders and, between 1900 and 1902, gliders that could actually hold a person. Finally, in 1903, they built a power airplane with a gasoline engine. On December 17, near Kitty Hawk, North Carolina, Orville Wright made the world's first flight in a heavier-than-air, gasoline-powered machine. This flight lasted only 12 seconds. But by 1908 he was able to stay in the air as long as an hour.

The original plane that made the first flight at Kitty Hawk can still be seen at the National Air and Space Museum in Washington, D.C.

Guglielmo Marconi (1874-1937)

Guglielmo Marconi was an Italian inventor and engineer. In 1895 he sent the first radio signals through the air. Before then telegraph signals had been sent through electric wires. Marconi used electromagnetic, or radio, waves to transmit signals. His system became known as "wireless telegraphy." In 1901 he succeeded in sending wireless signals across the Atlantic Ocean. Soon his equipment was being used to rescue people from sinking ships. Marconi continued making important advances in wireless communication. His work contributed greatly to the growth of radio broadcasting.

Helen Keller (1880-1968)

Helen Keller lived to be 88 years old, and except for her first two years she saw and heard nothing. If you are blind and deaf, you also cannot learn to speak by yourself. When she was seven, a wonderful woman named Anne Sullivan came to teach her. She used the sense of touch to reach the child's mind. She taught her the words for objects that the little girl could feel by using an alphabet of touches. She tapped out the letters on Helen's hand. Helen then learned to speak and write, and she eventually went to college.

Helen Keller traveled, wrote books, and worked tirelessly for other people with disabilities. She became famous all over the world. She was a shining example of the ability to overcome severe handicaps to live a productive life.

The Empress T'zu-hsi (1835-1908)

T'zu-hsi was one of Emperor Hsien Feng's concubines. When she bore him a son she became his favorite. At the time of the emperor's death she stole his royal seal. Without the seal, documents could not be properly signed. This stopped plotting courtiers from taking over the monarchy. T'zu-hsi governed China while her son was small. In 1875 the boy died of smallpox. She appointed her sister's son, Kuang Hsu, as the next heir. When he was 21, and could rule as emperor, she still had great influence at court. He tried to introduce reforms, but she made him her prisoner.

T'zu-hsi encouraged the Boxer rebels because she wanted China to return to the days before Europeans interfered with its politics. She loved to act in plays. People said that she looked as though she was always on the stage.

When the time came for her to die, she saw to it that her prisoner, Kuang Hsu, died first. She appointed the two-year-old Pu Yi as her successor. He was the last emperor of China.

American Firsts

1900   An automobile advertisement appeared in a national magazine.
First woman astronomer employed in the U.S. Naval Observatory, Washington, D.C.
First postage stamps issued in book form.

1901   A.C. Bostwick was first to drive a car faster than a mile a minute.
The hormone adrenaline was discovered.
A.E. Taylor was first person to go over Niagara Falls in a barrel.

1902   First Tournament of Roses football game played, Pasadena, Calif.
First international woman suffrage association founded, Washington, D.C.
Theodore Roosevelt was first President to ride in an automobile, Hartford, Conn.

1903   J.D. Sebring made the first home run in a World Series game, Boston, Mass.
M.L. Walker was the first black woman to serve as a bank president, Richmond, Va.
First railroad operated by an electric third-rail system went into operation, Penn.

1904   Radio distress signal established.
Ice-cream cones sold, Louisiana Purchase Exposition, St. Louis.

1905   An air-conditioned factory opened, Gastonia, N.C.
First balloon landed on a building, Toledo, Ohio.
Forest fire lookout tower built and watchman service started, Greenville, Me.

1906   Oscar S. Straus was first Jewish member of a President's Cabinet.
Bank that stayed open day and night opened, New York City.

| 1907 | A.L.R. Locke was first black to win a Rhodes scholarship.
Electric washing machine marketed, Chicago.
The first movie was made in Los Angeles. |

| 1908 | Bibles first placed in hotel rooms, Iron Mountain, Mont.
Indirect electric lighting demonstrated, Manchester, N.H. |

| 1909 | First coin with portrait of a President issued.
A.J. Hoffman patented a steam-operated pressing machine. |

New words and expressions

The English language is always changing. New words are added to it, and old words are used in new ways. New inventions, habits, and occupations cause people to introduce new words. Some of them are included in this list of words and expressions that first appeared or came into popular use in the 1900s.

adman	medicine show
ailurophobe	recessive
airspeed	right wing
bloc	rip cord
bonehead	Rocky Mountain
borderline	spotted fever
buffer zone	scrimmage line
bughouse	septic tank
disc brake	turtleneck
garage	wireless
Girl Guide	world power
grandfather clause	world war
holding company	worthwhile

How many of these words and expressions do we still use today? Do you know what they all mean?

Glossary

abandon: leave completely.

cavalry: soldiers on horseback.

Cossacks: horsemen in the Russian Army.

culprit: someone guilty of a wrongdoing or crime.

deception: trickery or fraud.

dwindle: shrink, become gradually smaller.

eruption: process of erupting, or blowing up. A volcano erupts when it suddenly and forcefully releases lava, hot rocks, or steam.

excommunicate: to cut a person off from taking part in church rituals.

flagship: ship that has the admiral on board.

horizon: line at which earth and sky seem to meet.

irrigation: process of supplying land with water by artificial methods, usually to water crops.

isolation: the condition of being alone, staying out of the affairs of other countries.

journalism: collection and preparation of news for presentation in newspapers, magazines, radio, and television.

legation: official house and offices of diplomats in a foreign country.

mandate: the right to control or administer, usually a country or territory.

monopoly: exclusive control of a commodity or service, a trust.

pavilion: an ornamental building, usually in a park or garden.

persecution: harassment and harsh treatment, especially on grounds of religion or race.

petrified forest: an area of ancient trees that have become stone.

piecework: work that is paid for according to the number of units finished.

skyscraper: very tall building.

slum: overcrowded and unhealthy housing.

snow blindness: irritation and sensitiveness of the eyes to bright light, brought on by too much exposure to the sun reflected from ice or snow.

sweatshop: a factory or workshop where poor people worked for long hours and very little money under very poor conditions.

trophy: prize.

wireless telegraphy: the sending of sound signals by radio waves.

Further Reading

Cairns, Trevor. *Twentieth Century.* Lerner, 1984

Carey, Helen and Greenberg, Judith. *How to Read a Newspaper.* Watts, 1983

—*How to Use Primary Sources.* Watts, 1983

Deery, Ruth. *Earthquakes and Volcanoes.* Good Apple, 1985

Duncan, Michael. *How Skyscrapers Are Made.* Facts on File, 1987

Epstein, Samuel and Epstein, Beryl. *Tunnels.* Little, Brown & Co., 1985

Falkof, Lucille. *William H. Taft: Twenty-seventh President of the United States.* Garrett Education Corp., 1990

Ford, Barbara. *The Automobile: Inventions That Changed Our Lives.* Walker & Co., 1987

Harris, Jacqueline L. *Henry Ford.* Watts, 1984

Keller, Helen. *The Story of My Life.* Airmont Publishing Co.

Meyer, Nicholas E. *Magic in the Dark: A Young Viewer's History of the Movies.* Facts on File, 1985

Reynolds, Quentin. *The Wright Brothers.* Random House, 1981

Schroeder, Alan. *Booker T. Washington.* Chelsea House, 1992

Stefoff, Rebecca. *Theodore Roosevelt: Twenty-sixth President of the United States.* Garrett Education Corp., 1985

Sullivan, George. *Famous Blimps and Airships.* Putnam, 1988

Tames, Richard. *Guglielmo Marconi.* Watts, 1990

—*Marie Curie.* Watts, 1991

Index